MW01229021

The Giving Cliff

The Giving Cliff

by
Craig C. Harris

The Giving Cliff

Copyright © 2022 by Craig C. Harris

All rights reserved. No part of this book may be reproduced in any form or by any mechanical means, including information storage and retrieval systems, without permission in writing from the publisher/author, except by a reviewer who may quote passages in a review.

All images, logos, quotes and trademarks included in this book are subject to use according to trademark and copyright laws of the United States of America.

ISBN 979-8-218-01645-6

All rights reserved by Craig C. Harris.
Printed in the United States of America.

Dedication

I would like to dedicate this book to Our Lady of Fatima. Ever since I venerated her in August 1998 at St. Martin de Porres Catholic Church in Boulder, Colorado, she has interceded in my life. I have consecrated myself to the missions she has wanted me to accomplish. This book, with its forewarning and education about the impending Giving Cliff, was wholly inspired by her. Any and all profits from this book will be donated to Fatima Garden of Colorado.

Table of Contents

The Giving Cliff:

… the impending challenge for Catholics (and Christians) when the churches reach the financial point of no return, resulting in the closing of our churches beginning within the decade and continuing to accelerate thereafter.

Foreword

I met Craig Harris in 2017. He and a mutual friend came to my house, and it was the beginning of a great friendship. I'd like to share a little about the author of this book. Craig is one of the most ingenious and active minds I have ever run across. An entrepreneur at heart, his perception and perspective on the world and on life is something we all need more of. His infectious enthusiasm and out-of-the-box thinking, just like his Catholic faith, are inseparable from his very large heart.

When Craig asked me to write the foreword for this book, I wasn't surprised. He often sees things others don't, and this request was no exception. His approachable nature and knack for conversation has endeared him to many in his community and in business. He started the longest-running restaurant in Boulder County in 1994. This was after discovering the rings around Neptune in 1982 and receiving his graduate degree in Astronomy and Astrophysics from the University of Colorado.

Among his many accomplishments, he is also a problem solver. Having run many successful businesses over the years, he has helped dozens of charities and causes and has raised four children with his wife, Mary. He has certainly seen his fair share of challenges, but that would be for another time.

He has been a member of the Catholic community in Boulder County since 1982, and he joined the Knights of Columbus in 1985. His love for the Catholic Church, along with his faith and devotion to Our Lady of Fatima, has always kept him looking outward, looking for how his gift of life can help further the cause of the Church. An avid traveler, he has attended mass and visited Catholic parishes all over the world and has noticed an alarming trend.

This book is going to challenge you. It will inform you of this future and cause you to reflect on what the Catholic faith truly means to you. Are you proud of the Catholic faith and all the traditions of the Catholic Church? Are you proud of the history of the Church and its universality across all nations, races, languages and cultures?

Are you proud of the apostolic lineage unique to the Catholic Church? Are you proud of the charity work, the apostolates, the hungry that are fed, the homeless who are cared for and clothed, and the children who are educated in the parish schools? I know I am.

The Catholic Church is not perfect; but it does more good for people in more locations and in more ways globally than any other religion or faith community. This impact is not just external; it is also internal and personal.

In Craig's new book, The Giving Cliff, there are two types of Catholics addressed: those who have been Catholic all their lives and those, like me, who have come into the Church. For life-long Catholics, (often called cradle Catholics), so much is taken for granted. For the new Catholics, everything is bright, interesting and relevant—the richness of the faith, the incense, the music and hymns, the liturgy of the word and the liturgy of the Eucharist.

Long-time Catholics often know what to do or what to say but may not remember why. New Catholics appreciate the faith more directly because it is all new, fresh, exciting and personal. Regrettably, it is part of human nature to not see what is often right in front of our noses.

Familiar things are taken for granted, and this includes all the different ways the Catholic faith enriches our lives every day. Whether you are a life-long or new Catholic, how would you value its importance to your life? It is incalculable. It is an amount so large we could never pay it back. It is an amount reflected in the sacrifice of Jesus.

Think of it! We can trace the origin of our faith back to Jesus and the apostles. That's the "Apostolic" part we say in the Creed at every Mass; it's not just a traditional phrase. G.K. Chesterton calls tradition the "democracy of the dead." In simple terms, this means we should respect and consider what the people who came before us did and why they did it.

What did those in your parish do for the parish before you? In almost every parish in the country, their ancestral parishioners certainly saw the future, or there wouldn't have been one! They considered, long after they had died and received their eternal reward, who would live and worship there.

These were the people who constructed the buildings, funded the expansion, built the schools or funded the scholarships—all to get more of God's children into Heaven. It wasn't just for their families and friends, but also for souls who did not yet exist. They started the food banks and ministries, helped the homeless and funded other parish needs.

The Catholic Church and its parishes were an integral part of their lives. These past parishioners lived and loved in your parish just like you do today. What they did before you allowed this parish to become a part of your lives.

Consider some of those similarities between

this parish and the Catholic Church that are so common, so expected, so presupposed, so ingrained in your life and the lives of your families, that you just assume them. Equally as important, what does the future look like?

How do you see your parish and the Catholic Church being a part of your future? Do you look forward to the Lenten Friday Fish Fry—you know ... the steaming-hot fried fish that burns your tongue and the extra napkins for the hush puppies? Maybe it's the feast days and picnics celebrated at the parish, or just the weekly coffee and donuts in the mornings after mass, where you always see your friends and other members of the parish community.

How many weddings have you celebrated at your parish, maybe even your own? How many do you expect to attend in the future? Weddings lead to children and grandchildren, then baptisms and christenings, First Communions and Confirmations. These events and sacraments weave a rich and important thread into who we are, and if undone would see all areas of our lives separate and fall apart.

Now, picture your community without an abundance of parishes, without the number of churches and priests and without the enumerable gifts of God's graces. Picture your parish— the one where you celebrated the marriages and the baptisms of your families and friends— CLOSED.

What if it permanently shut its doors because it couldn't afford to pay the monthly expenses necessary to keep them open? Imagine if this same church was boarded up with the lights off, the candle out and Christ no longer present in the tabernacle. Imagine a chain-link fence around the property and some of the stained-glass windows broken from neglect or vandalism.

How would that make you feel? Have you ever passed by a church like that? Have you ever considered what happened to cause such a tragedy? How could the parishioners have let that happen? What are the people in that parish doing now?

Now, ask yourself what you would do. Would you drive an hour to the nearest parish for weekly Mass? If you're a daily Mass goer, would you drive there every day? Would you get up an hour earlier because you now have a 50-minute commute instead of a 10-minute drive? What would you do on Fridays during Lent? Would you drive an hour, one way each week, for the Fish Fry?

What would this mean for you and your family's Easter and Christmas schedules and traditions? How would you feel knowing that your children or grandchildren would not be able to receive the sacraments in your parish because it would be closed? What if a spouse or close friend was dying and in need of Anointing of the Sick (extreme unction), and the nearest parish was an hour away?

Would you drive the extra distance to receive reconciliation or just live in your sin without the grace of absolution? The lives and eternal lives of so many that would be drastically changed is hard to fathom.

What would you say to future parishioners if they asked you what you did to save the parish? You could plead ignorance. You could easily say you had no idea that the parish would run into financial troubles and shut its doors. However, after reading The Giving Cliff, you could no longer plead ignorance. Once completed, you will know the why, the when, and most importantly, how to stop it.

For over forty years, Craig has applied his unique perspective to understand the current challenges that face each Catholic parish and those of other Christian denominations. Through his out-of-the-box problem solving skills and devotion to Our Lady of Fatima, he has created a unique and inspiring solution to the problem he discovered.

This book is about both the impending problem and finding a solution to avoid a future none of us want to see.

—Randy Opp
Author, *Wealth Basics: 15 Principles to Financial Freedom*

Prologue

Craig Harris makes a compelling case for the future needs of our Church. Those who regularly take responsibility for supporting the Church are often hampered by a litigious society. The Giving Cliff helps the common parishioner find a way to fit in and contribute. Craig talks about tithing and almsgiving in a general way. My intention is to give some depth.

Jesus uses the word "tithe" twice in Luke's Gospel. Both times, he challenges the immoral actions of the Pharisees. They are using this good biblical practice in the wrong way. As good as tithing is, it is not a substitute for bad intentions.

Once our intentions are purified, Jesus then recommends we should not neglect tithing. The tithe (10%) was used to support the operations of the priests and the temple. Our modern day application is to use the tithe for the upkeep of the parish church.

Separate from tithing is almsgiving. The assistance to the needy and the poor are the focus of almsgiving. Both almsgiving and tithing are challenges to the average Catholic. A half or quarter of a tithe is where some people start. To give nothing is not an option.

A mature Catholic knows that giving is a requirement of a Christian. How and when we start is open to a variety of styles and approaches. Craig has come up with a permanent solution to solve the financial problem without continually adding funds after the initial commitment. Your giving will be perpetual even after you have passed. The Giving Cliff is an approach that should give us all a moment to ponder God's plan for ourselves and for our loved ones.

—Rev. Andrew Kemberling
Author, *Making Stewardship a Way of Life*
OSV 2009

Chapter 1
The Giving Cliff

The Giving Cliff is a point of no return. The baby boomer generation is one of the biggest and wealthiest demographics in our history. They currently provide the lion's share of financial support for the Church. As their population decreases, so does that financial support, leading to the inevitable closures of our cherished parishes.

To put it another way, when the percentage of deceased baby boomers reaches the critical mass point, there won't be many of them remaining to support the Church's financial obligations. Churches will no longer have enough money flowing in via tithing, forcing them to shut their doors. This is The Giving Cliff.

How long will it take to get to the precipice? That is up to you.

The concept of The Giving Cliff has been recognized for the last 20 years. Because of this, archbishops and bishops around the country have established financial mandates for local parishes with two main goals.

The first mandate was for each parish to save enough money to sustain 6 to 12 months of liquidity, working capital, and to weather unforeseen storms and decreases in tithing. I have been privately informed that less than 5 percent of churches and parishes have accomplished this mandate over the last 20 years.

Many parishes live from collection basket to collection basket, just like families living from paycheck to paycheck. To put it bluntly, most parishes are fundamentally poor. Sure, they have beautiful buildings and beautiful grounds; but many parishioners don't appreciate all the loans, groundskeeping, maintenance, utilities and payroll requirements which add substantial costs to their monthly operating budget.

The second mandate was to establish a legacy endowment account (LEA) for each individual parish. However, almost every parish is drastically underfunded. Consider this example: A parish has $1 million in a money market account earning 5% interest, paying $50,000 per year. Almost everyone considers that to be a lot of money and security.

Now, consider that the average operating budget of a parish is between $1.5 million and $2.0 million annually. $50,000 will not go very far. To emphasize once again, in a short period of time there will not be enough surviving baby boomers to keep tithing amounts at current levels. There will not be enough money to keep parish doors open, resulting in as much as 40 to 70 percent of churches closing over the following decade.

It's hard to comprehend, and even harder to write down, but the year would be 2031—nine years from now! We'll be reaching the point of no return sooner than we think, so we need to implement the solution ASAP and at full throttle or we will be part of the problem.

Let's step up, be counted and say *Not on my watch!* We will not allow our churches to fail after 2,000 years.

Chapter 2
Are You Proud to Be a Catholic?

Are you proud of all the programs, rites and traditions we have in the Catholic Church? For us cradle Catholics, too much has been taken for granted. For those who are converts, they appreciate more about the faith than we do because they have made the choice and have taken the time to learn.

There are so many prayers and traditions available to us which help shape our lives, such as the Angelus, Guardian Angel prayer, Novenas, prayer before meals, the morning offering, the Divine Mercy chaplet, the surrender novena, and most importantly the daily rosary.

There are also the many prayers of blessings and intercession. The richness of the Catholic church, the seven Sacraments (especially Baptism, the Eucharist, Confession, Confirmation and Matrimony) are such a blessing.

We see our sons and daughters getting married in a real sacramental ceremony at Mass, celebrating and receiving God's blessings to us through His sacraments. The marriage ceremony takes an hour, not five minutes at a justice of the peace. Baptisms welcome our children into the faith.

Catholic funeral rites and burials help prepare souls to ascend to eternal life and be received by God. The saints themselves help us by interceding on our behalf. My favorite example is Saint Anthony, the patron saint for lost things, whom I call upon more often than I'd like to admit.

By our actions and deeds, we make God the forefront and center of everything we do, recalling James 2:14-26—faith without works is dead. By attending daily Mass, receiving the Eucharist, the actual body and blood of our savior, and having the gifts of confession, there are so many significant events and sacraments the church offers us that we take for granted.

If 50 to 60 percent of Catholic churches were gone, how would that affect our day-to-day lives? What if it took you over an hour to travel to the nearest Mass or confessional? What if you couldn't receive daily or weekly Communion because there weren't enough churches?

Imagine how this world would be changed if half the Catholic and Christian churches were gone. How much would that impact the poor and the homeless?

That's why we need to stand up NOW! That's why we've got to take action TODAY! That's why we MUST do our part to make sure The Giving Cliff won't happen on our watch after surviving 2000 years of success. I do believe God is watching, so let's do this!

Chapter 3

The Causes

First, I would like to acknowledge that the pressures and attacks on Christianity and the Catholic Church throughout history have filled volumes. However, I am only addressing a small section of causality, but it's something each of us can actually change. What could have caused this, and why are we facing The Giving Cliff?

The first thing to recognize is that baby boomers have accumulated more money than any other generation in history, but they are all nearing the end of their lives. In many cases, upon their deaths, they leave their wealth to their children.

However, their children (Generation X) do not spend money in the way their parents would have, in part because they don't have access to the wealth-building vehicles of the previous generation. Gen Xers don't have access to the many retirement resources (pensions, strong home equity, etc.), and they tend to have higher debt due to inflation, college loans, family bills, mortgages, etc.

Therefore, it falls to the remaining baby boomers to ensure their own resources are utilized and allocated in the way they would like, since Gen Xers are more likely to allocate their funds in different ways.

Another challenge facing churches is inflation and the rising costs of everything: groundskeeping, maintenance and staff salaries. These rising costs will continue to put pressure on the budgets and financial management of parishes across our country.

Currently

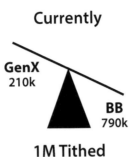

GenX
210k

BB
790k

1M Tithed

In summary, when the largest generational group passes on, there may not be a succeeding generation that continues funding the Church in the way baby boomers have so generously given.

The key to preventing The Giving Cliff is to find a solution that will sustain the financial lifeblood of the Church. That solution is the Perpetual Tithing Movement.

Chapter 4

Numbers and Trends

Let's get into some of the numbers around the problem. I love asking questions, so I'm going to ask you some. Take the time to cover the next few lines of the page so you can legitimately ask yourself the two questions. Give your answer before you uncover ours.

Question 1: Which population do you think tithes more to the Church ... 55-year-olds and over or 35-year-olds and younger?

Answer: Those 55 and older tithe more.

Question 2: Of all the money tithed to the Church, what percentage comes from the 55-and-over group?

Answer: 79% of all money tithed is from the 55-and-over group!

Only 7.1% of all money tithed is from those who are 35 years old and younger. Another critical component to watch for is attendance. The demographic numbers might be arguable, but no one can deny that attendance is falling everywhere.

All you need to do is look at your own faith community. Regarding the past 50 years, ask yourself if there are more or fewer people attending church. What will happen to the 55-and-older population over the next 20 to 25 years?

Next Decade

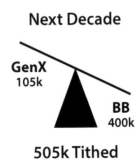

505k Tithed

Covid mandates certainly contributed to them all staying away. I believe it's prudent to assume the worst and hope for the best; this is especially true in finance.

When you assume the worst situation, you are at least prepared for a negative scenario. If the best happens, you're in a much better position. Whether one blames parenting or the Church or influences from many societal sources, the conclusion is still the same: less participation means less financial support for the church through tithing.

Two Decades

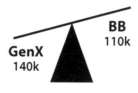

250k Tithed

The Perpetual Tithing Movement (PTM), explained in Chapter 12, buys time so that churches have the finances to stay open, giving the Holy Spirit and Our Lady of Fatima more time to get people back into the Church.

The last thing we want to witness is 40 to 70 percent of all churches being closed between 2035 and 2050. Many of those will be our own churches where we married our families, baptized our children and grandchildren, and perhaps buried our loved ones.

Without a miracle, it will be impossible to fund the repurchase of those lands, churches and other buildings by 2060. One of the lessons of the PTM is that its success is independent of the number of people remaining in the pews during those dark times.

Community Built Together, Forever

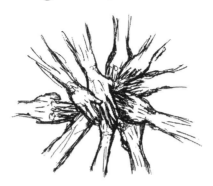

Chapter 6
Community Based

Let's analyze the history of giving and of generosity, and even the history of building and sustaining churches. In the old days, about 100+ years ago, churches were built by their communities.

Everyone contributed to the construction of the buildings; they were community events. If you were highly skilled, you donated your skill in that area. If a few folks were totally unskilled, like me, they would still donate their time, even if it was mixing the cement or bringing food to support the skilled workers.

Everybody participated! It may have taken decades to build a church, but much of the funding, materials (and certainly the time) were donated by the parishioners. This kept overall costs down; and everyone had the distinction of contributing their blood, sweat and tears to the building of the churches.

Everyone across multiple generations invested wholeheartedly in whatever way they could. Thus, it was much more community oriented and made it possible for every parishioner to contribute.

Over time, lawyers and wealthy donors got involved; then inflation, interest and long-term debt complicated the financial landscape. Nowadays, it costs millions of dollars to build one church. Only money and contractors are furnished—not the community labor of the past.

The intense pride of participating in the building of churches that would stand for hundreds of years, beyond your children and grandchildren, is gone.

The Perpetual Tithing Movement is the solution that brings to the table mass participation. Most people will be able to financially afford to participate in something that will be around for hundreds of years.

PTM is unique. Even if someone has never been financially successful, with assistance he/she can create resources and become a source of funding that will lead to the financial security of their church, parish or charity—forever. Yes, FOREVER! How is this possible?

PTM utilizes multipliers, which cost as little as $30, $100 or $150 per month and could avoid The Giving Cliff altogether. A price point of $100 per month would make the solution within reach by almost everyone, even if they have never been financially successful.

We'll cover some of the details in the next few chapters.

One
&
Done

**Cumulative
Gift**

Chapter 7
Some Definitions

One & Done giving is when a person simply donates money once. They put money in the basket, write out a check or go online. No matter how big that donation is, there is no recurring or residual component. It has been given only once and can be used only once.

That One & Done gift is wonderful and more than most will do, so God bless you. However, there's an issue with the One & Done giving method. A donor must be financially capable enough to give in the first place, and in today's economy that's a big issue.

I believe there are many people who have very big hearts who would love to be more generous and give more than 10 percent of their income. Unfortunately, most of them may never be financially successful enough to contribute with One & Done. It's very difficult to give financially when you don't have anything. Please keep in mind that I'm referring to the giving of money, not the giving of your time or gifted talents.

When a gift has a perpetual component, it is not given only once (One & Done); rather, it continues to be given every year forever. This now touches the infinite, and maybe even a little of the eternal.

Perpetual

Cumulative Gift

Chapter 8
One & Done vs Perpetual Tithing

Let's contrast the One & Done method to that of The Perpetual Tithing Movement. Imagine you won a million dollars, then you gave 10% to the church ($100,000). Congratulations for your generosity! You may have helped with new pews, paving a parking lot, or even helped a homeless family find a house through a church's charity organization.

What would your generosity have looked

like had you chosen Perpetual Tithing? If you took the same $100,000 from your $1M winnings, you could still give half of it ($50,000) directly to the church for their immediate needs. The remaining $50,000 could be gifted using PTM, which would generate over $1.5 million over time.

Did you catch that? A $50,000 One & Done donation could turn into a $1.5 million donation using The Perpetual Tithing Movement. From your $100,000 donation, the Church receives $100,000 with One & Done. With PTM, the Church receives $1.5 million. Which would you rather give the Church? This is why PTM is so effective.

Here's another example. What if God informed you that you were going to pass away next week? What are the chances you could write a donation check to your church for $100,000 and have it clear?

I would presume not many people would be capable of doing that because their money is often tied up in their homes, stocks and other assets.

Conversely, you'd have to be very financially

successful to consider giving the church $100,000. Yet, for about $100 a month through PTM, most people can be within reach of giving $100,000 to the church in a perpetual and permanent way.

The Perpetual Tithing Movement empowers everyone to be part of the solution—the solution that will avoid The Giving Cliff.

To be clear, this should be something in addition to your current tithing. Reducing your normal tithing will jeopardize the already strained Church financials. The PTM is more like giving alms, which is something above and beyond regular tithing.

As in the story of Cain and Abel, we want to give from our first fruits in gratitude to God; and in this case, to keep His churches open long after we pass and allow the Holy Spirit and Our Lady of Fatima to work.

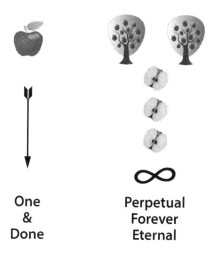

One
&
Done

Perpetual
Forever
Eternal

Chapter 9

More Benefits of Perpetual Tithing

When you donate a perpetual gift, you touch the eternal and realize the remarkable power of PTM. You begin to understand Matthew 25:14-30, the parable of the talents and God's request to multiply the gifts He has given us.

The amount of the gift is inconsequential because it will be given every year, forever and ever, long after you have passed. Further, it will be a shining example for your children and friends, who, from your example, may personally choose to do the same.

Whether your motivation is to establish a scholarship at a school or a grant for your parish or seminarians, the charity you choose will be empowered to continue because of the funds YOU have gifted to them. By your decision, these charities and parishes can avoid The Giving Cliff and continue their work.

You may wish to donate anonymously. If so, God bless you. You may name it on behalf of your child, your parents or anyone else you wish. The money can be donated in their honor or memory; it's all customizable.

Personally, I think it's awesome to empower people and to allow them to express the generosity they've always had—to make a reality of what only the financially successful have been able to do.

The solution has been created. The heavy lifting and conceptualization has been done. All you have to do is decide how much you want to commit per month. How big of a legacy do you want to be remembered for?

More importantly, when asked, how many times will you have multiplied the talents loaned to you by God?

Chapter 10

The Power of Perpetual

Here's a personal example of the power of Perpetual. My son is a physical education teacher and the head coach of Holy Family High School's track & field team. How likely would it be for a high school PhysEd teacher to accumulate enough money on his salary to establish a full scholarship fund at Holy Family High School in Broomfield, Colorado, where tuition is over $15,000?

The answer is: zero chance! Not just zero,

The Ripple Effect

**One small change
can have an enormous impact.**

Chapter 11
Ripples

I believe God evaluates us by how many ripples we make during our lives. Ripples continue long after a stone has reached the bottom of the lake. My definition of a ripple is when you have made a relationship better because of your participation or contribution. How many ripples have you made in your life? We will only know this answer when we meet God face to face, but it's worth pondering.

How many ripples will you have made after

you pass? Anyone who knows me can tell you I'm not satisfied with just making ripples. I want to make waves, but not just medium waves. I want to make tsunami waves—one the most powerful forces of nature, and I want to empower as many of you to do the same.

Consider this question: can you count the number of seeds in an apple? Yes, you can; but can you count the number of apples in a seed? No, you can't. Each seed can produce a tree, and each tree produces many apples. And each of those apples has many more seeds and more potential trees and apples.

Through The Perpetual Tithing Movement, you are touching immortality and the infinite. Through PTM, you are able to give beyond your own lifetime. The amount of people you can impact becomes infinite.

Imagine you are in heaven. Someone finds you there and thanks you for that scholarship or that church which would have closed had it not been for you. Because of that revitalized church, he or she was saved through their youth group. Just imagine.

Chapter 12
Solutions

Here are some of the blessings created by participating in the Perpetual Tithing Movement:

PTM enables everyone, in any financial situation, to participate in bringing back that spirit of community.

PTM becomes a permanent solution to preventing The Giving Cliff. The baby boomers would primarily be funding these LEA accounts, providing permanent year-in year-out working capital for their chosen parishes and charities. This would be 80 to 90 percent of their entire budget, independent of the number of parishioners in the pews.

For most of us, PTM enables us to institutionalize our giving. This is done through our guaranteed legacy contributions derived from the interest on legacy endowment accounts (LEAs). These in turn are distributed forever, per your instructions, because of the very nature of perpetual tithing.

PTM is an answer to the mandates parishes have been charged with by their bishops—6 to 12 months of working capital (cash) and establishing a legacy endowment account (LEA). Over the past 20 years, most parishes have created legacy accounts, but few have much money in them.

A unique benefit of PTM is that hundreds of small endowment accounts would feed into the parish's accounts instead of one massive parish legacy account. This structure has many benefits.

In nine years, The Giving Cliff will reach the point of no return. Nine years will pass in a blink of an eye. That's why we MUST take massive action to prevent this from occurring.

That's why I'm soliciting your support in getting the word out to all parishes at the grassroots level. That's why I've written this book to help communicate the basic components. I have shared the pointed facts of The Giving Cliff, what has contributed to it, and provided a solution to stop this catastrophic event.

The Perpetual Tithing Movement is easy and something everyone can do. We need all of you to allow the Holy Spirit to work in your parishes and your dioceses and to allow us to speak directly to your parishioners. We ask you to schedule evening events at each parish where we can educate your community about The Giving Cliff, why and when it will occur, and how each of us can play a role in preventing it.

Now is the time to act! This program means nothing unless you make the time to act today. Call or email us, and a member of the PTM team will review your situation. Find out what level of commitment best suits you and how you can multiply the talents God has given you to stop The Giving Cliff from occurring.

When I meet Saint Peter and Jesus, and they ask me, "Craig, what did you personally do to save our Church?" I know what my answer is going to be. "I did everything possible to stop The Giving Cliff on my watch."

During your next prayerful moment, holy hour or when in adoration, ask yourself what your answer should be.

We look forward to personally speaking to your parish or community.

Made in the USA
Columbia, SC
31 August 2022

65530997R00036